Obesity and the Media

Frances O'Connor

rosen publishing's
rosen
central®

New York

To Madeline, Anton, and Jack—three most beautiful children

Published in 2009 by The Rosen Publishing Group, Inc.
29 East 21st Street, New York, NY 10010

Copyright © 2009 by The Rosen Publishing Group, Inc.

First Edition

Library of Congress Cataloging-in-Publication Data

O'Connor, Frances.
Obesity and the media / Frances O'Connor.—1st ed.
    p. cm.—(Understanding obesity)
Includes bibliographical references and index.
ISBN-13: 978-1-4042-1769-0 (library binding)
1. Obesity in mass media. I. Title.
P96.O23O26 2009
362.196'398—dc22

                                            2007049700

Manufactured in the United States of America

Contents

Introduction

Obesity, a condition in which a person weighs too much for his or her body type, has reached epidemic levels. In fact, former U.S. surgeon general Richard Carmona, M.D., has called obesity "the greatest threat to public health today." According to the American Medical Association (AMA), in 2007, more people died from obesity than from AIDS, all types of cancer, and accidents combined.

Unfortunately, obesity currently affects many young Americans. The Centers for Disease Control and Prevention (CDC), an organization that tracks diseases in the United States, uses body mass index (BMI) to determine if an adult is overweight or obese. BMI, calculated using a person's weight and height, is used because, for most people, this number correctly identifies their amount of body fat. For children and teens, however, the CDC uses the labels "at risk of overweight" and "overweight" for above-normal BMI. The reasoning for this is that the condition can change by the time a person becomes an adult. The BMIs of children and teenagers are also slightly different than for adults because there are normal differences in body fat between boys and girls at different ages. A child or teenager is usually considered overweight if he or she is in the ninety-fifth percentile of weight on the age and gender growth chart. For example, if a twelve-year-old girl weighs more than 95 percent of girls her age and height, the doctor would determine that she's overweight.

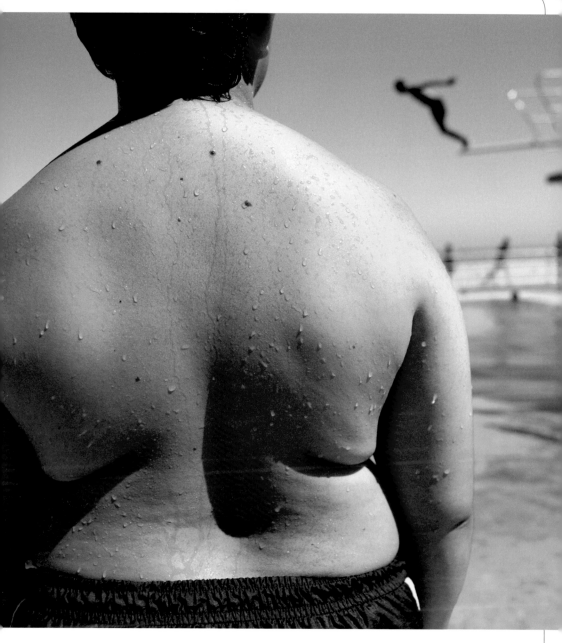

This teen is overweight, meaning that his level of body fat is above normal for his height. Overweight children or teens have a higher risk of being overweight or obese as adults, and they can face a number of health problems.

Obesity is worrisome because it brings with it many other health problems. In the past five to ten years, doctors have noticed that overweight children and teenagers experience the same problems that previously only affected overweight adults. According to Dr. Jennifer Lindstrom, director of the Bariatric Surgery Center at Albany Medical Center in Albany, New York, pediatricians have noticed that very overweight children and teenagers are now battling high blood pressure, knee and back pain, type 2 diabetes, and fatty liver. The AMA agrees. Involved with an expert committee studying and assessing overweight children, Dr. Cecil B. Wilson, chair of the AMA, said, "Overweight children tend to have health problems more commonly found in adults like diabetes, high cholesterol, and high blood pressure."

Doctors and parents are very concerned, and they wonder why obesity is reaching epidemic proportions. Luckily, the cure to obesity is pretty well known—a healthy diet and regular exercise. The causes of obesity need to be examined, however, so that the condition can be avoided in the first place.

Doctors and fitness experts say that a major cause of obesity is the amount of time that children and teenagers spend sitting in front of the television and the computer. Another cause is a diet that is high in fat, salt, and sugar, including those in processed foods like fast food, potato chips, and frozen meals. Doctors also point to portion size: Americans eat bigger meals today than they did just ten years ago. Plates and cups have changed sizes, too, in order to accommodate people's larger meals.

In addition, media plays a role in today's obesity rates. TV shows, movies, and Web sites advertise specifically to children and teenagers. It may seem unbelievable that advertising can cause people to be overweight. After all, viewers don't have to do what

Television commercials for fast food and snack food air at times when kids are most likely to be watching television—after school and on Saturday mornings.

advertisements say. However, ads make obvious (as well as subtle) suggestions about what to eat, buy, wear, or how to live. Fast-food advertising, for example, has been proven to affect how people eat. Today, food advertising appears in all kinds of media—on billboards, on the sides of buses and at bus stops, in Web pop-ups, in magazines and newspapers, on the back of concert tickets and supermarket receipts, on the radio, on television, and in the movies. Food advertising causes people to remember a catchy saying like "I'm Lovin' It!" for McDonald's, or a character like the Colonel, who brings Kentucky Fried Chicken to mind. It is this kind of advertising that makes people want to eat the food

Even very young children are affected by advertising. Above, a girl eats a Wonka chocolate bar at a showing of the movie *Charlie and the Chocolate Factory*.

that's marketed to them. Unfortunately, a lot of fast food and snack food is high in fat, sugar, and salt—all of which causes weight gain. If children and teenagers get the message from advertising that this food is good and should be eaten on a regular basis, it can help lead to obesity at a young age.

In 2004, the American Psychological Association (APA) studied the effects of television advertising on children. Doctors found that kids *do* change their habits because of what they see on TV. In a press release about the report, Dr. Brian Wilcox, one of the heads of the study, said, "They [children, especially under eight years of age] are easy targets for commercial persuasion." He also said, "This is a critical concern because the most common products marketed to children are sugared cereals, candies, sweets, sodas, and snack foods. Such advertising of unhealthy food products to young children contributes to poor nutritional habits that may last a lifetime and be a variable in the current epidemic of obesity among kids."

It is no wonder that parents and doctors are worried. When children and teenagers watch television, they are getting positive messages about many unhealthy food choices. The media that children and teenagers watch and pay attention to the most is the same media that companies use to sell their unhealthy food. It is important to be aware of what messages companies hope viewers will pay attention to. Most often, it's a message that a certain product will make life better or more fun. Where certain kinds of food are concerned, it is a good idea to get a variety of messages, not just one. Read on to understand more about the connections between obesity and the different kinds of media in America today.

Chapter 1

How Food Is Advertised and Marketed

A movie is just a movie, right? A story that you watch for two hours and then it ends and you go back to your own life. But when you are watching a movie, do you ever wonder, for example, where you could get a pair of jeans like the ones a character is wearing? Or, have you ever gotten hungry thinking about what the characters are eating? If so, you are not alone. Believe it or not, there are a lot of people hoping that you *will* notice and *will* want to buy, use, and eat these things.

Today, movies and television shows are becoming more and more like long commercials. Companies such as Coca-Cola, Kentucky Fried Chicken, McDonald's, and Nike pay directors a lot of money to have their products appear numerous times on-screen. (Repeated viewing of products will make sure that viewers get a strong message.) These companies want kids to believe that

Fast food is often placed in important or funny movie scenes. Above, Coca-Cola and Kentucky Fried Chicken products appear in *Talladega Nights: The Ballad of Ricky Bobby*, starring John C. Reilly *(left)* and Will Ferrell.

buying the product will make their lives better somehow. They hope that by having a likable character use their product, kids will want to use their product, too. Or, companies may hire marketers or a marketing agency, whose job it is to make people want to buy the companies' products. Although they are not the salespeople who actually sell the products, they try to figure out how to make them look appealing to children and teenagers. For example, marketers may give away samples or coupons for their products. They do this because they know that once kids try a product, chances are they will want more of it. They hope that kids will ask their parents to buy it for them. Or, better yet, they hope that kids or teens will save their own money to buy the product. If kids or teens buy a certain product with their own money and they like how it looks or tastes, it is likely that they will continue to buy the product. Companies hope that these young customers will then keep buying the product for years to come. Furthermore, companies hope that when these kids grow up, they will buy the product for their children as well. This idea is called brand loyalty.

PRODUCT PLACEMENTS AND PLUGS

There are two major ways in which marketers help companies to get the attention of a consumer. In each case, the consumer is being exposed to a product without being told that it was put there for advertising purposes. The first, and most common, way is through product placement. Marketers place a specific product, like a food or a brand of clothing, in a form of entertainment media such as a movie, television show, music video, or video game. The company that makes the product pays the movie directors, television producers, or video game creators to have characters eat, drink, or use actual products, like a Burger King Kids' Meal, for example, or a bottle of Gatorade. Sometimes, a company even pays to have its product's logo appear on a poster in a movie's background. The marketing agency figures out the coolest, funniest, or most noticeable way to put the product in a scene so that the audience pays attention to it. The product becomes an important part of a scene, and the audience never knows that they're actually seeing a paid advertisement.

The second way in which companies get their products noticed by consumers is through a product plug. It is the same idea as

Coca-Cola has sponsored *American Idol*. As a result, its name, logo, and products are featured prominently on the show. From left to right, Simon Cowell, Paula Abdul, and Randy Jackson are all drinking Coke during *Idol*'s fifth season, above.

product placement—the product appears and becomes an important part of a scene. However, the director doesn't get any money. The director puts a product in a scene because he or she thinks that the product is cool or it fits in with a certain character's life. For example, characters might drive Volkswagen Beetle cars or drink Coca-Cola soft drinks because they are young and hip and love being charged up and on the go. As with product placement, a product plug repeatedly shows a product so that the audience gets a positive idea about it. In the case of a product plug, however, the company hasn't paid for it. The director likes the product so much that he or she puts it in an important place for free.

In the Movies

Do you wonder just how many products are appearing in movies these days? Check out the Web site: http://www.brandchannel.com/ brandcameo_films.asp. A company called Interbrand compiles this Web page, which lists products that appear in new movies. For example, did you know that *Harry Potter and the Order of the Phoenix* features Ecko Unlimited gear and Nike sneakers? Or, that *Night at the Museum* shows characters using Apple computers, wearing Nikes, drinking Pellegrino water, and driving Ford, GMC, and Toyota cars? Interbrand uses this information to figure out ways to get more products in front of kids in each and every scene of a movie, TV show, or video game.

MARKETING DIRECTLY TO CHILDREN AND TEENS

One reason that the obesity epidemic has been getting worse in recent years could be due to the amount of marketing that is currently aimed at kids. It is only in the past twenty to thirty years that advertising and marketing companies have worked with products that appeal specifically to kids. In fact, advertising and marketing agencies used to work only on making things look good to adults, who made and spent much of a household's money. They thought that kids didn't influence how adults spent their money. However, starting in the 1980s with the movie *E.T.: The Extra-Terrestrial*, which featured a Reese's Pieces–loving alien, advertisers and marketers discovered that if certain kinds of candy or food are placed in popular kids' movies, then kids will be more likely to ask their parents for them. This seemed to work more than if kids had just seen a commercial for the product on television. Marketers and food and clothing companies thought that this was a smart way to start advertising. Today, they spend approximately $3 billion a year putting products in children's movies.

Web sites like MoviePlacement.com make money by offering their product placement services to directors. They pay directors to use certain products in movies, and they suggest the best ways to show the products in order to get the audience's attention. In return, they get money from the company that makes the products. For example, a potato chip company will pay MoviePlacement.com to sell the idea of using its potato chips to a movie director. When the director agrees to use the potato chips in a scene, the potato chip company makes money because the audience will be more likely to buy its potato chips.

A Web site called ProductPlacement.biz has a newsletter and news articles about successful product placements in movies and on television. Marketers can read these materials and see what has been successful in selling products to people of different ages.

IS FOOD A PRODUCT?

Most people probably don't think of food as a product because they eat it every day. Chances are, you have never seen a commercial about having baby carrots "your way," or a commercial with the slogan "Spinach: I'm Lovin' It!" In fact, most people probably haven't seen commercials for fruits or vegetables at all. Can you name two different brands of lettuce or carrots? You probably

Fruit and vegetable growers don't need to use catchy sayings or cartoons to advertise their food. Consumers must eat these foods to stay healthy.

can't. The reason you can't name different brands isn't because they don't exist or that you haven't seen different brands at the supermarket. It's because carrot growers haven't spent loads of money on advertising. They don't think of their food as a product. They don't need to. They know that kids and teenagers have to eat fruits and vegetables in order to stay healthy and grow, so they don't worry that no one will remember their product's name. They're confident that they won't go out of business, even if their food isn't put in fancy packages. For good health reasons, they know that people are customers for life.

Who Makes Unhealthy Food Look So Good?

Makers of junk food and fast food know that if they succeed in capturing a young person's attention, then he or she will most likely buy their product for a long time to come. Therefore, they pay advertisers millions, sometimes billions, of dollars each year to try to get—and keep getting—the attention of kids and teens.

Many people are involved in creating advertisements that appear on television, the Internet, a billboard, or elsewhere. It takes a lot of hands to make the food look so mouth-wateringly good, including those of:

- **The art director**, who sets up food for photos and commercials. He or she may spray hamburgers and french fries with hairspray, cover them in glue, or even paint them just to make them look yummy and fresh.

- **The photographer**, who sets up special lighting and backgrounds to make food look good enough to eat. He or she may use lighting to hide details like the fat that oozes from hamburgers. Lights may also be used, for instance, to get the shine on top of a gooey candy bar just right.

- **The marketing executive**, who makes sure that in a movie or television program, a favorite character bites into a specific product just as he is getting an e-mail from the girl of his dreams. The marketing executive works for the food company, making sure the company's product looks perfect (and perfect to buy).

People who make fast food and junk food such as potato chips, candy, and soft drinks know that their products are not an essential part of a healthy diet. They know that they have to advertise with clever sayings, cool commercials, and product placement and plugs in order to encourage people to add these unhealthy products to their diets. They need to create a market and a fake need for the food that one's body doesn't actually need. McDonald's, for example, spends more than $1 billion each year advertising its food in the United States alone.

HARMFUL MARKETING AND ADVERTISING

Although it is tempting to think that advertising in movies, on television, and on Web sites like Nick.com isn't a big deal, recent evidence proves that this kind of advertising actually encourages children to choose unhealthy food. In August 2007, the *Archives of Pediatrics & Adolescent Medicine* published a study about fast-food advertising and kids. In the study, researchers put chicken nuggets, a hamburger, baby carrots, milk, and french fries into a McDonald's wrapper or bag. They then put the exact same food in a different wrapper. Researchers gave the kids the two sets of food at the same time and had them taste both. Most of the sixty-three kids tested said they preferred the food in the McDonald's wrappers, even though the food in both sets of packaging was exactly alike. What was the biggest surprise of the study? The kids were ages three and five. If you think that young children don't pay attention to advertising, ask your younger siblings or cousins if they know who Ronald McDonald is. Most likely they do, even if they've never eaten at McDonald's

Kids around the world know McDonald's because of the chain's hamburger-loving clown, Ronald McDonald, who stars in its advertisements.

before. This is because they have constantly seen McDonald's on TV or in the movies.

HEALTH EFFECTS OF FATTY FOOD

According to the American Academy of Pediatrics (AAP), fatty food can cause teenagers to develop dangerously high cholesterol and blood pressure levels, which, in turn, can cause heart attacks. Fatty food can also lead to kids developing type 2 diabetes, which previously was a disease that only occurred in adults after many years of eating a poor diet. Joint problems can develop, too, from the strain of carrying around an unhealthy amount of weight. A diet of fatty food can bring about sleep apnea, a condition in which breathing stops while a person is sleeping.

If kids are excited to eat McDonald's at the young age of three, and they keep eating this fast food on a regular basis, then advertisers have been successful—they have gained some loyal customers from very early on. But these advertisers have also been successful at luring a group of kids into the danger zone of obesity and serious health problems.

Chapter 2

How the Media Markets Unhealthy Food to Kids

O besity-causing fast food and junk food are sometimes advertised in places like the movies and in video games. They are also successfully advertised in more common ways. This advertising, which is all around, can affect how kids and teens eat.

People frequently see unhealthy food advertised in television commercials. According to a 2004 study by the American Psychological Association (APA), advertisers spend more than $12 billion a year on advertising messages for children and teenagers. According to a Kaiser Family Foundation study, the average American child watches more than forty thousand television commercials per year. That's forty thousand chances for companies to show kids their products! Most of these forty thousand ads are for candy, cereal, soda, and fast food. They're

Funny commercials, like this ad that shows a boy getting sucked into a Pepsi bottle, make young audiences remember some drinks more than others.

usually not for food that encourages good health. Nor are these commercials for products that encourage a lifestyle of regular exercise. The 2004 APA study found that kids are more likely to want unhealthy food after seeing these commercials.

When a commercial is successful in making the audience want a product, its success can result in the audience developing very unhealthy habits. Companies hire advertising agencies to make commercials that are entertaining and interesting. In these commercials, everyone is having a good time. A company will hire an advertising agency to come up with a saying or a funny idea that kids will remember. For example, the McDonald's phrase "I'm Lovin' It!" is simple and catchy. It helps to make a McDonald's product hard to forget. The advertising agency can also come up with other products that the company can distribute for free to make sure that kids will return to the restaurant. For a promotion starting a few years ago, for example, McDonald's gave away Teenie Beanie Babies with Happy Meals. Record numbers of people bought the meals just to get the toys. McDonald's also offers toys that are based on a movie that has just been released in theaters. When this happens, the sales of Happy Meals go up. Toy giveaways are different from product placement, but they are just as successful. The makers of a movie don't need to place the fast food in the movie itself because they know kids will want a Shrek action figure, for instance, if they have seen the movie. It's a win-win situation for both the fast-food restaurant and for the movie director.

It is also common for movie and cartoon characters—which young kids will easily recognize—to "star" in snack food commercials. Foods such as Cheez-It crackers and fruit snacks use characters like Spider-Man and Dora the Explorer so that kids will connect the food with the character or television show that they like. From there, kids are more likely to ask for this food when they are in the supermarket. The report explains that the more commercials children watch, the more likely they are to be overweight.

AT WHAT AGE DOES FOOD MARKETING TO KIDS BEGIN?

Advertising agencies and marketers hope that children's positive ideas about certain products will start when they are as young as two years old. They also hope that these good feelings will last

Spider-Man Says Buy Your . . .

The following well-known characters have been used to advertise high-calorie foods:

Spider-Man	fruit-flavored snacks
Dora the Explorer	Teddy Grahams snacks
SpongeBob Squarepants	gummy candy
Harry Potter	jellybeans
Shrek	Cheez-Its
The Fairly Odd Parents	gummy candy
X-Men	hard candy
The Incredible Hulk	popsicles
Transformers	Burger King Kids' Meal
Spyro the Dragon	Wendy's Kids' Meal
Barbie	McDonald's Happy Meal

for a lifetime. James McNeal, a well-known expert on product marketing, wrote a book titled *The Kids Market: Myths and Facts*. The book is based on McNeal's thirty-five years of researching kids' behavior. In this book, he explains to marketers and advertisers how they can introduce kids to products such as candy bars. McNeal spent years studying children in order to figure out how their parents and friends help them make decisions. He also studied how much money kids actually have and what they do with their money. He studied what labels get young children's attention in the supermarket. McNeal even figured out that kids usually start going to the supermarket with their parents when

Snack-sized food giveaways like this one by Kellogg's are ways that companies try to get kids interested in their products.

they're two months old; therefore, he's able to give advertisers information on how to catch babies' attention. In *The Kids Market: Myths and Facts* and his other books, McNeal tells advertisers how kids get their parents to buy things they want to eat and how kids begin to save their own money for treats they want.

Food Marketing in the Past

James McNeal isn't the only person who has studied young kids to figure out how to get them to want certain foods at an early age. This business idea started in the 1950s with Walt Disney, the creator of Mickey Mouse. In his book *Chew on This*, author Eric Schlosser explains how Disney gave different companies permission to use Mickey Mouse's image on snacks, clothes, toys, and books. His idea, which is called synergy, was that if Mickey Mouse's image appeared on a lot of different products, then Mickey Mouse would link all of the products together in people's minds. That way, Disney could advertise several products at the same time. Once kids had seen Mickey Mouse on television, Disney knew that they would recognize him on T-shirts and boxes of cereal. Soon, Disney began to sell the rights to all of his cartoon characters to cereal and snack companies. He started making a lot of money this way. He even thought to create a place where people could go to meet their favorite cartoon and movie characters. There, people could also buy food items and clothes with their favorite characters on them. Disney built Disneyland and Disney World as a business plan to market all the Disney characters to families near and far.

Soon, other businesspeople started using the same idea for their products. Ray Kroc, the founder of the McDonald's fast-food

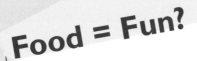

Food = Fun?

Fast-food slogans often sound like messages that a parent or coach would give. They can sound like rules for having a great life. However, these messages are really just sayings that try to sound cool or powerful so that the person buying the product can feel like a superhero or an adventurer. The following are some advertisers' messages:

Do the Dew!	Mountain Dew soda
Have It Your Way!	Burger King
You're the Boss	Burger King
Break Out of the Ordinary	Butterfinger candy bar
Do What Tastes Right	Wendy's
Put a Smile On	McDonald's Happy Meals
Obey Your Thirst	Sprite soda
Make a Run for the Border	Taco Bell

corporation, tried to have his hamburgers and french fries sold at Disneyland and Disney World. Walt Disney refused, wanting everything—even the food—at his theme parks to have only Disney characters on them. As a result, Kroc decided to create a hamburger-loving clown named Ronald McDonald to advertise McDonald's food. He introduced the character in television commercials. He thought that as with the Disney characters, once kids saw the friendly character, they would want to buy the product that the character was advertising. Kroc also knew that when a child wanted to go to a restaurant like McDonald's, the whole family would come along as well. Like Walt Disney's idea of Disneyland, Ray Kroc began to create McDonald's playlands

Companies often use pictures of kids on their packaging and make individual "fun pack" or "snack pack" servings to make their food more kid-friendly.

and parks so that families could come and spend the day. He knew that the larger the crowds, the more food they would buy.

FOOD MARKETING IN TODAY'S MEDIA

Advertisers and marketers use many different kinds of media to get messages about food products to kids and teens. Advertisements appear in magazines and on the Internet in pop-up windows and on Web sites. Today, there are marketing agencies that only market products to children. Just a few years ago, marketing agencies for kids didn't exist because kids didn't use as much media. Now, kids use the Internet to read books online and do their homework and research projects. Many kids have their own computers. Agencies such as Creative Consumer Concepts in New York City focus on studying kids and parents so that they can market products to kids in popular ways. These marketing agencies survey kids to find out about their favorite activities, as well as their likes and dislikes. They run focus groups, where they invite kids to play with a new toy or try a new snack food. These kids are then asked to tell the researchers what they think about the product. Researchers sometimes ask the kids to keep diaries about their activities, including how much time they spend online. Some companies even take kids' brain scans in order to get an idea about what kinds of products they will like! For example, in *Chew on This*, Schlosser talks about how Chupa Chups, a lollipop maker, uses brain research called "neuromarketing." Neuromarketing studies kids' brain activity as they watch different commercials. If a certain part of the brain reacts strongly, it means that they liked the commercial.

Kids are excited when they see familiar characters like Shrek on items in the super-market. The ogre-green filling in the above snack is Shrek-specific, meant to make kids want to eat what their favorite character might eat.

These uses of media to get kids' attention are pretty clever. However, winning kids' attention with regard to food high in saturated fat, sugar, and calories is a recipe for potentially disastrous weight gain and overall poor health. An organization called Commercial Alert watches how marketing agencies target kids. It is unhappy with all of these messages and commercials directed at kids, and it calls obesity a "marketing-related disease." The company's Web site states, "In the U.S., the #1 public health disaster of our times is the epidemic of marketing-related diseases that corporations have inflicted upon us. This epidemic is manufactured by people who have decided that the health of other people is less important than their own desire to make money." Whether or not you agree with the idea that marketers are just trying to get kids to spend money, it is important to think about how to respond to so many commercials and messages.

Chapter 3

Negative Portrayal of Obesity in Media

If you watch American movies and television, you will often see characters eating fast food and snack food. Strangely, they never appear to gain any weight from eating this unhealthy food. It is very rare for a movie or TV character to be overweight or look unhealthy.

Why aren't more overweight kids and teens portrayed on television and in the movies? The Centers for Disease Control and Prevention (CDC) reports that results of the 2003–2004 National Health and Nutrition Examination Survey (NHANES) show that approximately 17 percent of American children and adolescents between the ages of twelve and nineteen are overweight. The study also reveals that the number of overweight teens and preteens in this age group increased from 11 percent to 17 percent in just the past decade. The number of

Characters on TV shows are often shown eating snack food or fast food when they get together, as if this is what friends always do.

Growing Portions

Commercials, television programs, and movies show people eating portions that are much bigger than what nutritionists would call "normal." It is unrealistic to eat the way that people do on television or in the movies without gaining a substantial amount of weight and being generally unhealthy. It is important to know about normal portion sizes in order to understand what healthy food choices actually look like. Some recommended food-serving sizes are below.

Food Group	Normal Portion Size	Size
Meat and other protein	3 ounces of meat, fish, or poultry	A deck of cards
	2 tablespoons of peanut butter	A ping-pong ball
Grain products	1 cup of cereal flakes	A fist
	1 pancake	A music CD
Dairy products	2 scoops of ice cream	A baseball
Vegetables and fruit	1 cup of salad greens	A baseball
	1 baked potato	A fist
	½ cup of fresh fruit	Half a baseball

overweight kids and teens is continuing to rise quickly. However, this truth is not being carried over into Hollywood because, as a society, America is uncomfortable with the idea of obesity. Americans do not like looking overweight or unhealthy, and they know that being very overweight is unhealthy. Yet, they keep taking in advertised messages that imply that eating fast food will make them better or happier people. These are truly mixed messages.

TELEVISION AND MOVIE PORTRAYAL OF OBESE PEOPLE

When obese or overweight people *do* appear in entertainment media like television or the movies, they typically are not treated fairly. The overweight character, who is almost always male, is often the funny guy or the best friend. He or she is usually not the popular kid or the person in which others have a romantic interest. The character is more like Nacho Libre (played by Jack Black in the movie of the same name), a guy who's lovable and funny, but still someone whom the audience is meant to laugh at. The message is that overweight people are not as important as thin people and their feelings don't need to be respected as much. This also gives the audience the message that being overweight is automatically funny. The characters eat too much, so their size is their own fault. Therefore, they deserve to be made fun of. A character such as Eddie Murphy's overweight wife in *Norbit* is a good example. She is portrayed as a disgusting and unlikable character. Most of the people she meets are scared by her weight, which she uses as a weapon to threaten them.

This depiction of the overweight and obese creates negative stereotypes of people who face weight problems, and it makes a

Movies like *Nacho Libre*, starring Jack Black, portray overweight characters as loveable "losers." This stereotype is often used in films to make fun of overweight people.

joke out of a serious health matter. In this way, movie and TV directors and writers are pretending that obesity isn't a real issue. They either ignore it by not showing any overweight characters, or they suggest that obesity is humorous in and of itself. In reality, the health issues that come from being obese are not at all funny. Obesity can cause heart disease, joint pain, type 2 diabetes, and other problems. As an audience, we have a responsibility to educate ourselves and learn ways to fight bad habits—and not watch media that makes fun of obesity.

A DIFFERENT PERSPECTIVE

The Lifetime channel movie *To Be Fat Like Me* contains typical Hollywood scenes of characters laughing at the overweight character and being mean to her. There is a surprising angle, however: the main character is a thin girl who is disguised in a fat suit. Based on a true story, this movie follows a high school–aged girl who decides to wear a fat suit to school under her clothing and make a documentary about how she's treated. She expects to be treated normally, but instead she becomes the center of people's attention in the hallway, in class, and especially in the cafeteria. *To Be Fat Like Me* shows her panic as classmates call her names and taunt her as she simply walks by. Viewers immediately see that it is painful to go from being thin to being overweight in our society. In real life, the girl quit her fat-suit experiment, which was a story for a magazine, after two days because she felt too embarrassed and upset by the negative attention that she was receiving. The movie's audience watches Americans' negative attitudes toward weight gain. Another movie that looks at stereotypes and feelings about overweight people is *Shallow Hal*.

Shallow Hal, a movie about a man who cares only about the physical appearances of women, starred Gwyneth Paltrow *(right)*, who altered her appearance by dressing in a "fat suit."

In the movie, actor Jack Black's character is vain and unfair to the women he meets. Through a bit of magic, though, the character falls in love with a beautiful young woman whom he sees as thin. Meanwhile, everyone else who meets her can see that she is overweight. As a result of his experiences, he gradually learns to be a kinder person and to accept people for who they are on the inside, rather than how they look on the outside.

Movies with these particular perspectives are quite rare, and they were written to show the importance of being kind to others. More frequently, however, movies that star overweight characters place them in the roles of "jokesters" or "losers."

Myths and Facts

Myth: Viewers are not affected by food or behavior shown on television or in movies.
Fact: According to the American Psychological Association (APA), kids often do make food choices based on what they see on television. Doctors who study kids have noticed that food advertising is very powerful.

Myth: The teen obesity epidemic is overly hyped. Not that many teens are actually overweight.
Fact: According to the Centers for Disease Control and Prevention (CDC), around 17 percent of American children and teenagers who are between twelve and nineteen years old are overweight. Overweight adolescents have a 70 percent chance of becoming overweight or obese adults.

Myth: There is no proof that media contributes to childhood obesity.
Fact: Studies have shown that media consumption plays a role in America's increasing childhood obesity rates. For example, children and teens who watch more than two hours of television a day are more likely to be overweight than those who do not.

Myth: The food industry only markets products to parents because they are the ones who decide what groceries to buy.
Fact: The food industry is increasingly marketing its products to children, who, in turn, influence what groceries their parents buy. Entire companies work to create catchy songs and link favorite characters to snack foods in order to get kids to want those foods.

Chapter 4

How the Media Today Is Helping to Fight Obesity

There are some positive signs that the media is being used to help stop the obesity epidemic. Today, people can turn on the television and watch shows like *The Biggest Loser* and *Celebrity Fit Club*, both of which feature overweight contestants competing to lose weight. The person or team that loses the most weight wins the contest—and often receives money and other prizes. This is a good example of how entertainment media such as television can be used in a constructive way. When you witness people working hard to lose weight, you are seeing their feelings and watching them change as people. It's an exciting way to share in their adventure. It can also be a great motivator, as well as a way to learn about the importance of diet and exercise.

Entertainment media like television can be used to fight childhood obesity in particular. In October

Television shows such as *The Biggest Loser* are examples of entertainment media that deal with obesity in a positive way. Viewers can watch people like Kelly Minner *(above)*, from the show's first season, work hard to lose weight and, in turn, feel inspired to begin their own exercise regimens.

2004, Nickelodeon, a popular kids' TV network, didn't air any of its programs for three hours in order to encourage kids to get off the couch. During the time it would have been on the air, the network estimates that 1.6 million kids would have been watching. That's a whole lot of children who were encouraged to go out and play! When Nickelodeon came back on, it broadcast a program about balancing television watching with exercising regularly. Today, it's pretty common to see TV characters exercising and eating well. *Sesame Street* has a lot of messages about healthy food and exercise, as does another popular kids' show, *Lazytown*. Shows for older children, like Nickelodeon's *Naked Brothers Band* and *Drake & Josh*, feature characters that play sports and have healthy lifestyles.

THE INTERNET AND OBESITY INFORMATION

The Internet has a number of sites that have information about fighting obesity for kids and teens. On its Web site, the California School Nutrition Association has a public-service announcement from actress Hilary Duff, who talks about eating well in the school cafeteria. It includes her thoughts on beauty: for instance, she says that makeup can only make a girl so beautiful; it's a good diet that does most of the work. To read more about Duff and find tips about fighting obesity, go to the California School Nutrition Association's Web site, StayFitEatRight.org.

Another helpful Web site that provides anti-obesity facts is MyPyramid.gov, which features the food pyramid. Click the "For Kids" link on the site's home page for solid health information about calorie consumption and exactly how much food from

Hilary Duff's partnership with the Stay Fit, Eat Right Web site, sponsored by the California School Nutrition Association, is an example of how the Internet can promote powerful, positive messages to encourage teens and children to be healthy.

Which Media to Tune Into?

Entertainment media:

- **Television:** Shows like *Sesame Street* and *The Wiggles* for very young children feature characters being active. Kids are encouraged to be active as well. For older kids, programs that encourage activities include *Naked Brothers Band*, *Drake & Josh*, and *Just Jordan*.
- **Video games:** Play games like Konami's *Dance Dance Revolution*, Wii's *Boogie* or *Tennis*, or EyeToy's *Kinetic*. With these games, you follow the computer's dance moves or make on-screen characters move by jumping and swinging in order to score points.
- **Movies:** Watch movies like *Bend It Like Beckham* and *Bring It On*. You might be inspired to join a soccer team, football team, or cheerleading squad.

News media:

- **Magazines:** Read *Sports Illustrated for Kids* or *Junior Scholastic* magazine, and decide which of the sports profiled appeals to you.
- **Newspapers:** Read the health section of your local newspaper and be sure to check out the fitness articles. They usually include helpful information such as where good hiking trails and parks are near you.

Web media:

- **Web sites:** Go to http://members.kaiserpermanente.org/redirects/landingpages/afd to play the Amazing Food Detective game. Or, go to www.mypyramid.gov/kids/kids_game.html to play the MyPyramid Blast Off Game. If you have a younger brother or sister, you can go to www.nickjr.com and look at the "Activity Finder" box for each day of the week. You can also click on "Games: Inside, Outside, and Online" to find rules for games like Dora's Soccer Obstacle Course and Blue's Clues Tag Football.

each food group is best. Kids can plug in their age, height, and weight, and get appropriate food and exercise information.

The National Institutes of Health (NIH) also has good information. Its "We Can! Ways to Enhance Children's Nutrition and Activity" Web site (www.nhlbi.nih.gov/health/public/heart/obesity/wecan) offers games and interesting facts for kids to learn the best ways to avoid unhealthy habits. One eye-opening section is "Portion Distortion" (http://hp2010.nhlbihin.net/portion/index.htm). Users can see how the portion size of foods such as bagels and spaghetti have increased in just a few years.

WEIGHT LOSS IN NEWS MEDIA

News media for kids and teenagers has begun to cover the issue of obesity. Magazines like *Time for Kids* and Scholastic's *Choices* now include more health articles. Just a few years ago, these magazines would not have had articles about kids who are trying to lose weight. Today, they focus on health issues that affect the current generation of kids and teenagers. Readers can find tips for balancing the stress of schoolwork and extracurricular activities with a routine that includes exercise and eating well.

Television news for kids has also begun to focus on obesity. In 2005, on the Nickelodeon channel's *NickNews*, former U.S. president Bill Clinton was interviewed about his health crisis. He described how his fatty diet resulted in the need for him to have heart surgery. Clinton talked about being overweight as a child and craving all the wrong foods. He continued to make unhealthy food choices for a long time. After having a heart attack, he realized that he must make better decisions about the food he eats. He lost weight and today, Clinton maintains a

45

Video games like Konami's *Dance Dance Revolution* can help people lose weight and have fun at the same time. Above, Terrance Jones plays the game in a New York City arcade.

proper diet and exercises regularly. He encouraged teens and children watching the *NickNews* interview to do the same.

Media often focuses its message on promoting unhealthy food. However, many kinds of media can be used to discourage bad habits and fight obesity. The epidemic that affects so many Americans can be stopped. It just means that children and teenagers should think about what they read, hear, and see in the media. There are some good and even great messages, if you know what media to tune into.

USING ENTERTAINMENT MEDIA TO LOSE WEIGHT AND STAY FIT

Parents often discourage their children from spending a lot of time playing video games because they feel it's not good for them. But some video games might actually help children lose weight. Video game makers know that one of the reasons children and teens are becoming obese is that they are sitting still in front a screen playing games for hours. So, they came up with a way to combine exercise with a media kids love. Called exergaming, this newly popular activity is a combination of exercise and video gaming.

Exergaming started in the 1980s, when a company called Autodesk developed an exercise bike that a user could ride through a virtual environment. If users pedaled fast enough, they would look as if they were flying through the air on the screen in front of them. This same company also developed *Virtual Racquetball*, a game where users could wear "eyephones." This headset allowed them to view themselves and opponents swinging racquets that would hit racquetballs into virtual reality. Atari soon followed, making an exercise bike that was attached to its game system. Nintendo made a power pad that users would step and jump on to control actions on the screen. These games were cool ideas, but they were too expensive for most people to purchase for their homes.

Video game technology has continued to get better—and cheaper. Fisher Price has introduced an exercise bike aimed at young children. Called Smart Cycle, it plugs directly into a television and comes with software than uses motion-sensing technology.

When Nintendo came out with Wii in 2007, it was an immediate hit with families. It includes an exercise package called *Wii Sports*, which contains golf, bowling, tennis, boxing, and baseball games. This system uses motion-sensing technology. Players can swing at imaginary balls and jump up and down to make on-screen characters move and score points. Users can also dance and sing with Wii's *Boogie* and *Karaoke* games.

PlayStation 3 and EyeToy are also popular systems on which people can play games that feature motion-control characters. The company Activision even has a *Dancing with the Stars* game that is similar to the hit television show. The game allows players to perform the same dance moves as the celebrity on the screen. One or two players can practice a variety of dance routines, from tangos to foxtrots, burning calories all the while.

Fitness clubs and gyms have started using similar media to get kids involved in exercise. Some health clubs have built-in "kidzones," where children and teens can use exergaming systems while their parents work out in another part of the club. A company called XRtainment Zone has created centers in the United States and Canada where kids can go to use these systems.

The Fisher Price Smart Cycle, which fitness guru Richard Simmons *(standing)* introduced in 2007, encourages kids to exercise and be active from an early age.

These virtual gyms, or exergaming centers, have programs where families can attend seven-week-long training sessions together.

KEEPING MEDIA'S ROLE IN PERSPECTIVE

All kinds of media play a big part in kids' and teenagers' lives. This is great because it means that these young people have access to information and ideas from all over the world. They can read on the Internet about any topic from alligators in the Amazon to zebras in Zimbabwe. They can hear or read about events that affect people within moments of when they occur. However, they can also hear, read, and see a lot of messages that can be unhealthy. It is important to remember that the media is a tool. It communicates many good messages. It also communicates messages that can lead to unhealthy lifestyles. To be a healthy person, one should look and listen carefully to the media's message, and then think about how it will contribute to a healthy life. The media is a great tool of communication if it is used carefully, and even greater if we think about how we will use it.

Ten Great Questions To Ask a Doctor

1. Can I trust that a food is healthy if I see characters eat it in a movie or on television?

2. Is a food good for me if I see a cartoon character I know on the front of the package?

3. Is there a certain time of day that most commercials on television target people my age?

4. What kind of food ads in movies and on TV should I question when I see them?

5. How can I tell if an energy drink and other advertised "energy-boosting" food products are truly healthy?

6. How can I tell if a food is really low in fat if I see it advertised that way on television or in a magazine?

7. After seeing a commercial for a new food product, where do I go to get more information on this product?

8. What resources can provide me with reliable exercise information?

9. What foods should I eat for a balanced diet?

10. What's the best way to fit exercise into my daily schedule?

Glossary

advertising industry The companies that make advertisements, which typically appear on the Internet, radio, and television; and in movies, video games, and public areas like bus stops.

body mass index (BMI) The number that the Centers for Disease Control and Prevention (CDC) uses to determine if a person is overweight or obese. This number usually tells a doctor the amount of body fat a person has.

epidemic Spreading more quickly and extensively among a group of people than expected; a serious disease that affects many people at the same time.

high blood pressure A condition, often caused by a diet that is very high in salt, where blood flows through the arteries at too fast a rate; also called hypertension.

influence To affect a person's thoughts or actions by using certain powerful words or pictures; to change someone's mind.

media Means of communication that reach a lot of people at once, like the Internet, radio, television, newspapers, and magazines.

nutritionist A medical doctor who is trained in the science of a healthy diet. He or she can help you make a healthy diet plan and can test your blood and organs for diseases that might prevent you from getting enough vitamins and minerals.

obesity A condition in which a person's weight is excessively high for his or her body type.

synergy When a company advertises a lot of products at once by having them linked together by one character or popular person.

target audience A specific group of people that a marketing or advertising message is targeting. This is often an age group, such as teens or tweens.

type 2 diabetes A condition, usually caused by obesity and lack of exercise, that causes the body to have trouble processing sugar, or glucose.

For More Information

Advertising Standards Canada (ASC)
175 Bloor Street East
South Tower, Suite 1801
Toronto, ON M4W 3R8
Canada
Web site: http://www.adstandards.com
Part of the Canadian advertising industry, the ASC sets standards
   for acceptable advertising. It helps make sure that ads are
   truthful, accurate, and fair.

Alliance for a Healthier Generation
55 West 125th Street
New York, NY 10027
Web site: http://www.healthiergeneration.org
This partnership between the William J. Clinton Foundation and
   the American Heart Association aims to eliminate childhood
   obesity and inspire healthy habits.

American Academy of Pediatrics (AAP)
141 Northwest Point Boulevard
Elk Grove Village, IL 60007
(847) 434-4000
Web site: http://www.aap.org
The Web site provides information on a number of health topics,
   including a section devoted to "Overweight and Obesity."

Center for Media and Democracy (CMD)

520 University Avenue, Suite 227

Madison, WI 53703

(608) 260-9713

Web site: http://www.prwatch.org

This non-profit public interest organization tries to catch unsafe
or unfair Web site, commercial, and magazine ads. CMD
looks at how media messages affect citizens' health.

Centers for Disease Control and Prevention (CDC)

1600 Clifton Road

Atlanta, GA 30333

(800) 311-3435 or (404) 498-1515

Web site: http://www.cdc.gov

This public health agency's Web site offers credible information
on a wide variety of health topics.

Children's Advertising Review Unit (CARU)

70 West 36th Street, 13th floor

New York, NY 10018

(866) 334-6272, ext. 111

Web site: http://www.caru.org

CARU is part of the Council of Better Business Bureaus, Inc. It
works in voluntary cooperation with children's advertisers to
ensure that their advertising is truthful and accurate.

Commercial Alert

P.O. Box 19002

Washington, DC 20036

(202) 387-8030

Web site: http://www.commercialalert.org
Commercial Alert aims to prevent commercialism from exploiting children, family, and community.

Media Awareness Network
1500 Merivale Road, 3rd floor
Ottawa, ON K2E 6Z5
Canada
(800) 896-3342 or (613) 224-7721
Web site: http://www.media-awareness.ca
This Canadian non-profit agency focuses on helping people understand how media and advertisers work, and how media may affect lifestyle choices.

Web Sites

Due to the changing nature of Internet links, Rosen Publishing has developed an online list of Web sites related to the subject of this book. This site is updated regularly. Please use this link to access the list:

http://www.rosenlinks.com/uno/obme

For Further Reading

Boutaudou, Sylvie. *Weighing In: How to Understand Your Body, Lose Weight, and Live a Healthier Lifestyle.* New York, NY: Amulet Books, 2006.

Dillon, Erin, ed. *Obesity* (Issues That Concern You). Farmington Hills, MI: Greenhaven Press, 2006.

Dudley, William, ed. *Mass Media* (Opposing Viewpoints). Farmington Hills, MI: Greenhaven Press, 2004.

Ford, Jean. *Diseases and Disabilities Caused by Weight Problems: The Overloaded Body* (Obesity: Modern-Day Epidemic). Broomall, PA: Mason Crest Publishers, 2005.

Gay, Kathleen. *Am I Fat? The Obesity Issue for Teens.* Berkeley Heights, NJ: Enslow Publishers, Inc., 2006.

Ingram, Scott. *Want Fries with That? Obesity and the Supersizing of America.* New York, NY: Franklin Watts, 2005.

Kirberger, Kimberly. *No Body's Perfect: Stories by Teens About Body Image, Self-Acceptance, and the Search for Identity.* New York, NY: Scholastic, 2003.

Levy, Lance, M.D. *Understanding Obesity: The Five Medical Causes.* Buffalo, NY: Firefly Books, Ltd., 2000.

Libal, Autumn. *Fats, Sugars, and Empty Calories: The Fast Food Habit* (Obesity: Modern-Day Epidemic). Broomall, PA: Mason Crest Publishers, 2004.

Libal, Autumn. *Social Discrimination and Body Size: Too Big to Fit* (Obesity: Modern-Day Epidemic). Broomall, PA: Mason Crest Publishers, 2005.

Metcalf, Tom. *Obesity* (Perspectives on Diseases & Disorders). Farmington Hills, MI: Greenhaven Press, 2007.

Nakaya, Andrea C., ed. *Obesity* (Opposing Viewpoints). Farmington Hills, MI: Greenhaven Press, 2005.

Owens, Peter. *Teens: Health and Obesity* (The Gallup Youth Survey: Major Issues and Trends). Broomall, PA: Mason Crest Publishers, 2005.

Schlosser, Eric, and Charles Wilson. *Chew on This: Everything You Don't Want to Know About Fast Food*. Boston, MA: Houghton Mifflin, 2006.

Tessmer, Kimberly A., Meghan Beecher, and Michelle Hagen. *Conquering Childhood Obesity for Dummies*. Hoboken, NJ: Wiley Publishing, 2006.

Bibliography

Action on Obesity. "Background on Obesity." Retrieved October 29, 2007 (http://www.actiononobesity.org/background.html).

Action on Obesity. "White Paper—Action on Obesity 2005." Retrieved October 2, 2007 (http://www.actiononobesity.org).

American Medical Association. "Experts Release Recommendations to Fight Childhood and Adolescent Obesity." eMaxHealth.com, June 9, 2007. Retrieved January 16, 2008 (http://www.emaxhealth.com/109/12824.html).

American Psychological Association. "Television Advertising Leads to Unhealthy Habits in Children; Says APA Task Force." February 23, 2004. Retrieved January 16, 2008 (http://www.apa.org/releases/childrenads.html).

Beecher, Meghan, Michelle Hagen, and Kimberly A. Tessmer, RD, LD. *Conquering Childhood Obesity for Dummies*. Hoboken, NJ: Wiley Publishing, Inc., 2006.

Campo, Paul. *The Obesity Myth: Why America's Obsession with Weight Is Hazardous to Your Health*. New York, NY: Gotham Books, 2004.

Centers for Disease Control and Prevention. "Childhood Overweight." Retrieved October 21, 2007 (http://www.cdc.gov/nccdphp/dnpa/obesity/childhood/index.htm).

Centers for Disease Control and Prevention. "NHANES Data on the Prevalence of Overweight and Obesity Among Adults: United States, 2003–2004 (PDF)." Retrieved October 26,

2007 (http://www.cdc.gov/nchs/products/pubs/pubd/hestats/ overweight/overwght_child_03.htm).

Centers for Disease Control and Prevention. "Overweight and Obesity." Retrieved October 25, 2007 (http://www.cdc.gov/ nccdphp/dnpa/obesity/index.htm).

Critser, Greg. *Fat Land: How Americans Became the Fattest People in the World*. New York, NY: Houghton Mifflin, 2003.

Deville, Nancy. *Death by Supermarket: The Fattening, Dumbing Down, and Poisoning of America*. Fort Lee, NJ: Barricade Books, 2007.

Ellin, Abby. *Teenage Waistland: A Former Fat Kid Weighs in on Living Large, Losing Weight, and How Parents Can (and Can't) Help*. New York, NY: Public Affairs Books, 2005.

Kaiser Family Foundation. "Kaiser Family Foundation Releases New Report on Role of Media in Childhood Obesity." February 24, 2004. Retrieved October 10, 2007 (http://www.kff.org/entmedia/entmedia022404nr.cfm? RenderForPrint=1).

Keeler, Sharon. "Teen Obesity and Family Environment." *Medical News Today*, August 15, 2005. Retrieved September 28, 2007 (http://www.medicalnewstoday.com/articles/29129.php).

Levy, Lance, M.D. *Understanding Obesity: The Five Medical Causes*. Buffalo, NY: Firefly Books, Inc., 2000.

Mayo Clinic Staff. "Weight Loss: Childhood Obesity." MayoClinic.com, March 31, 2006. Retrieved October 2, 2007 (http://www.mayoclinic.com/health/childhood-obesity/ DS00698).

Mayo Clinic Staff. "Weight Loss: Obesity." MayoClinic.com, May 9, 2007. Retrieved October 2, 2007 (http://www. mayoclinic.com/health/obesity/DS00314).

Nemours Foundation. "When Being Overweight Is a Health Problem." *Teens Health*, April 2007. Retrieved September 29, 2007 (http://www.kidshealth.org/teen/food_fitness/dieting/obesity.html).

Okie, Susan, M.D. *Fed Up! Winning the War Against Childhood Obesity*. Washington, DC: Joseph Henry Press, 2005.

Program for the Study of Entertainment Media and Health. "First Analysis of Online Food Advertising." The Henry J. Kaiser Family Foundation, July 19, 2006. Retrieved October 10, 2007 (http://www.kff.org/entmedia/entmedia071906pkg.cfm).

Schlosser, Eric. *Fast Food Nation: The Dark Side of the All-American Meal*. New York, NY: Harper Perennial, 2005.

Sears, William, M.D., Martha Sears, R.N., James Sears, M.D., and Robert Sears, M.D. *The Healthiest Kid in the Neighborhood: Ten Ways to Get Your Family on the Right Nutritional Track* (Sears Parenting Library). New York, NY: Little, Brown and Company, 2006.

Skloot, Rebecca. "Flabby Coverage." *Popular Science*, June 2005. Retrieved September 24, 2007 (http://www.popsci.com/popsci/science/40b40b4511b84010vgnvcm1000004eecbccdrcrd.html).

Tartamella, Lisa, Elaine Herscher, and Chris Woolston. *Generation Extra Large: Rescuing Our Children from the Epidemic of Obesity*. New York, NY: Basic Books, 2004.

Zhou, Kevin. "Flawed Media Coverage of Teen Obesity." *NewsHour Extra*, September 29, 2003. Retrieved October 1, 2007 (http://www.pbs.org/newshour/extra/speakout/editorial/obesity_9-29.html).

Index

About the Author

Frances O'Connor is a former New York City high school teacher. She started studying weight and obesity after noticing that many of her students were affected by this crisis. She is the author of five health and wellness books for children and teens.

Photo Credits

Cover, p. 1 (mannequin) © www.istockphoto.com/David Calichchio, (TV) © www.istockphoto.com/Ensa, (red carpet) © www.istockphoto.com/Baris Simsek; p. 5 © Karen Kapoor/Stone/ Getty Images; p. 7 © Mike Siluk/The Image Works; p. 8 © Frazer Harrison/Getty Images; p. 11 © Sony Pictures/Courtesy Everett Collection; p. 13 © 20th Century Fox Film Corp. All rights reserved/Courtesy Everett Collection; p. 16 © www.istockphoto.com/Richard Beebe; p. 19 © Mario Tama/Getty Images; pp. 22, 28 © AP Images; p. 25 © Jeff Greenberg/The Image Works; p. 30 © PR Newswire/Newscom; p. 33 Monty Brinton/© CBS/Courtesy Everett Collection; p. 36 © Kevin Winter/Getty Images; p. 38 © 20th Century Fox Film Corp./Everett Collection; p. 41 © NBC/Courtesy Everett Collection; p. 46 © Mario Tama/Getty Images; p. 49 © Erik Sumption/Sipa/Newscom.

Photo Researcher: Amy Feinberg

29.25   4/14/10

LONGWOOD PUBLIC LIBRARY
800 Middle Country Road
Middle Island, NY 11953
(631) 924-6400
mylpl.net

LIBRARY HOURS

Monday-Friday	9:30 a.m. - 9:00 p.m.
Saturday	9:30 a.m. - 5:00 p.m.
Sunday (Sept-June)	1:00 p.m. - 5:00 p.m.